MILITARY MISSIONS

SPECIAL OPS

BY NEL YOMTOV

EPIC

BELLWETHER MEDIA • MINNEAPOLIS, MN

EPIC

EPIC BOOKS are no ordinary books. They burst with intense action, high-speed heroics, and shadows of the unknown. Are you ready for an Epic adventure?

This edition first published in 2017 by Bellwether Media, Inc.

No part of this publication may be reproduced in whole or in part without written permission of the publisher.
For information regarding permission, write to Bellwether Media, Inc., Attention: Permissions Department, 5357 Penn Avenue South, Minneapolis, MN 55419.

Library of Congress Cataloging-in-Publication Data

Names: Yomtov, Nelson, author.
Title: Special Ops / by Nel Yomtov.
Description: Minneapolis, MN : Bellwether Media, Inc., [2017] | Series: Epic: Military Missions | Includes bibliographical references and index. | Audience: Ages 7-12.
Identifiers: LCCN 2016007731 | ISBN 9781626174399 (hardcover : alk. paper)
Subjects: LCSH: Special forces (Military science)–United States–Juvenile literature. | Special operations (Military science)–Juvenile literature.
Classification: LCC UA34.S64 Y68 2017 | DDC 356/.160973–dc23
LC record available at http://lccn.loc.gov/2016007731

Printed in the United States of America, North Mankato, MN.

TABLE OF CONTENTS

UNDER ATTACK!

A team of United States Army **Green Berets** surrounds a house in Iraq. A **terrorist** group is keeping **hostages** there.

TURKEY

SYRIA

IRAN

IRAQ

JORDAN

N
W · E
S

SAUDI ARABIA

KUWAIT

The Green Berets get ready for action. Then they run in!

The enemy fights back.
But the Green Berets are
stronger. They quickly take
the building.

The prisoners are inside.
Nobody is hurt. Then they
all hurry back to safety!

THE MISSION

Special ops teams are small groups of highly trained fighters. They have the most dangerous jobs in the U.S. military.

BLENDING IN

Team members often have beards and long hair. This helps them work secretly in other countries.

The teams often work in enemy **territory**. Their missions are top secret.

These forces often make quick strikes on the enemy. Sometimes they gather **intelligence**.

Special ops teams also train local armies. They help other countries fight terrorism.

OTHER SPECIAL OPERATIONS MISSIONS:

- Hostage rescue
- Search and rescue
- Peacekeeping
- Security assistance

REAL-LIFE SPECIAL OPS

What: Easter SEAL Rescue

Who: U.S. Navy SEAL Team Six

Where: Indian Ocean, off the coast of Somalia, Africa

When: April 12, 2009 (Easter Sunday)

Why: Rescue the captain of the cargo ship *Maersk Alabama*, which had been taken hostage by three pirates

How: Navy SEAL snipers shot the three pirates and rescued the captain

Captain Phillips

Maersk Alabama

THE PLAN

Special ops forces are trained to use **machine guns** and **carbines**. They also shoot **sniper rifles** and pistols.

M2 machine gun

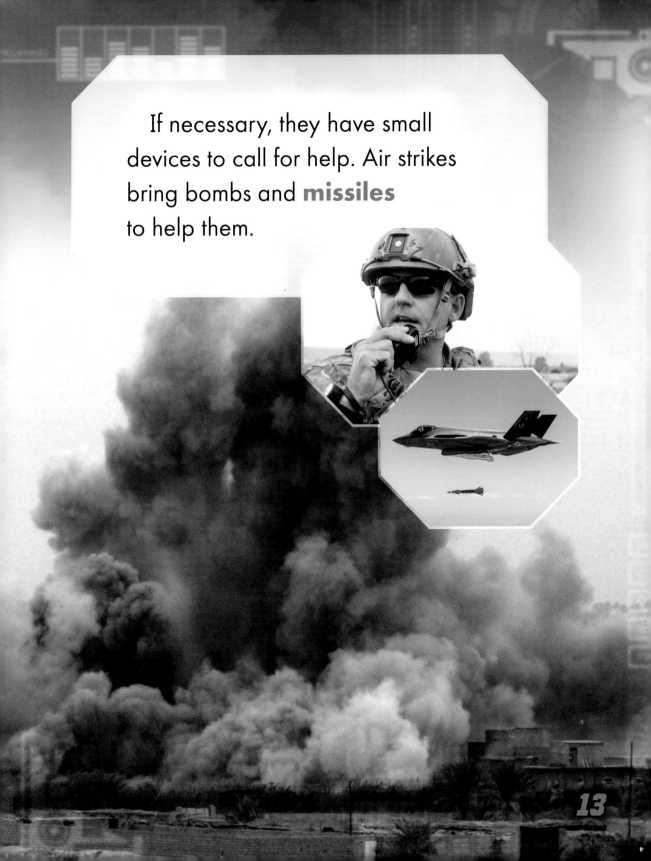

If necessary, they have small devices to call for help. Air strikes bring bombs and **missiles** to help them.

Special ops forces move quickly and quietly. They often **parachute** into missions.

Near water, they sometimes SCUBA dive to avoid being seen. Kayaks help them glide silently into the action.

SPECIAL OPS EQUIPMENT AND GEAR

M4 carbine

M240 machine gun

M9 pistol

Barrett M107
sniper rifle

FIM-92 Stinger missile system

THE TEAM

Some special ops teams focus on **raids** and quick strikes. Others fight terrorism and free hostages.

Different groups often work together on missions. They combine their skills to get the job done.

Members of special ops forces have many years of training. Many of them have special roles within their teams.

They learn how to fight in many conditions. They know to survive in the wilderness. They also know how to withstand being taken by the enemy.

A LOT TO LEARN

Military members usually have about eight years of experience before they join special ops teams.

SOLDIER PROFILE

A special ops member needs to have:

- Courage
- Excellent physical condition
- Intelligence
- Teamwork
- Loyalty
- Self-confidence
- Sense of duty

19

ACCOMPLISHED!

Special ops forces face dangerous missions. But their actions protect **innocent** people.

Their missions make the world a safer place.

A WORLDWIDE JOB

In 2015, U.S. special ops forces were working in nearly 150 countries around the world.

GLOSSARY

carbines—small, lightweight guns

Green Berets—specially trained soldiers in the United States Army Special Forces

hostages—people who are captured by a person or group that wants something in exchange for their freedom

innocent—not deserving to be harmed

intelligence—information about an enemy's position, movements, or weapons

machine guns—automatic weapons that rapidly fire bullets

missiles—explosives that are sent to targets

parachute—to jump from an aircraft with a parachute; a parachute is a large, umbrella-shaped cloth attached to someone to help them fall safely from the air.

raids—surprise attacks

sniper rifles—guns designed to be shot from hiding places

territory—an area of land owned by a group or a government

terrorist—a person who uses violence to try to get something

TO LEARN MORE

AT THE LIBRARY

Gordon, Nick. *Army Delta Force*. Minneapolis, Minn.: Bellwether Media, 2013.

Labrecque, Ellen. *Special Forces*. Chicago, Ill.: Raintree, 2012.

Slater, Lee. *Marine Force Recon*. Minneapolis, Minn.: ABDO Publishing, 2016.

ON THE WEB

Learning more about special ops is as easy as 1, 2, 3.

1. Go to www.factsurfer.com.

2. Enter "special ops" into the search box.

3. Click the "Surf" button and you will see a list of related web sites.

With factsurfer.com, finding more information is just a click away.

INDEX